R. M. Slaughter

Key to the Secret of Breeding

For sex with Horse, Jack, and Bull

R. M. Slaughter

Key to the Secret of Breeding
For sex with Horse, Jack, and Bull

ISBN/EAN: 9783337144562

Printed in Europe, USA, Canada, Australia, Japan

Cover: Foto ©Andreas Hilbeck / pixelio.de

More available books at **www.hansebooks.com**

KEY TO THE SECRET

— OF —

Breeding for Sex

—— WITH ——

HORSE, JACK AND BULL,

— OR —

How to Have a Male or Female Offspring,
as the Breeder May Desire.

Discovered after thirty-eight years experience and observation

— BY —

R. M. SLAUGHTER.

COMPILED AND EDITED BY

J. B. LAMKIN, Paris, Texas.

Sherman Printing Company.
Sherman, Tex.

INDEX.

PREFACE.

IN preparing this little volume for publication, I have tried to keep constantly before me the fact that the matter it contains must take its place in the ranks of the highest scientific production, and by its simple practicability hold its place there, or live the ephemeral life of many very splendid speculative theories. The principal thoughts therein contained, though clothed in language of my own, did not originate with me, but came to me through a chain of circumstances favoring much the nature of a providental maneuvre. In February of the present year, Mr. Slaughter, the original discoverer, or rather the rediscoverer, of the secret of breeding for sex, realizing his inability to prepare his work for publication, sought for some one to whom he could safely impart his secret, and associate with himself in its publication and management. Knowing personally Mr. R. B. Barber, resident with himself, of the Indian Territory, and a stock breeder, he opened to him in bonded confidence, his experiments and observations of the entire thirty-eight years which he had devoted to the subject, and gave Mr. Barber all the liberty that could be reposed in a confidential trust. Mr. Barber soon realized that his trust was of more than ordinary magnitude, and in order to treat it according to its demands would require some one more familiar with the laws of physical life than himself, and hence he felt the necessity of the assistance of a third man. Meeting Mr. Barber while pursuing my ministerial work, and giving him apparent satisfaction in answer to his questions on various subjects, he concluded he had met his man, and, with the same prudential guard, with which himself was bound he delivered to me his bonded trust. As a consequence it became necessary for me to meet Mr. Slaughter, who, at the instance of Mr. Barber opened to me fully his secret laboratory. How well these men have judged of my ability to handle a subject of such imposing and peculiar bearing, can be known only in the sequel. Twelve years previous to this, Mr. Slaughter, confidentially delivered to Mr. Geo. Coffman, a noted stock breeder of Collin county Texas, his secret from whom I gained much valuable information, the result of his continued tests for the entire twelve years in both his horse and jack breeding, mention of which is made elsewhere. Thus equipped I began the work before me, having as a farmer the greater part of my life, had some experience in stock breeding, and taken many observations from the law of reproduction, and the science of government reigning in both animal and vegetable kingdoms. I appreciate the value of the certificates of actual tests made by individual farmers, following the instructions of both Mr. Slaughter and Coffman, which certificates will be given their proper place in the body of this little volume, and which will from the beginning shield my work against the expected wreckage of an unsupported theory. I shall not offer in evidence the most plausible theory, indulged even, as a physiological fortress, without giving sufficient warning, to place the reader well on his guard. I shall endeavor from the beginning to the ending of this little work, to keep from it, any appearance of a literary or scientific romance, in the flowery field of ancient or modern thought, and deal with facts and common sense only. I am sure that my entire work will undergo a crucial analysis, and it will be right that it shall, announcing as it will, as a proven surety,

that which has long been set aside as the "improba-
ble." I cannot hope to offer a finished work in so
new a field, suggesting an appendix to the arduous
labors of the ancient philosopher and modern scientist.
But I do hope that, with this key which will pass
from our hands, some more skillful and penetrating
mind will take and apply it to the removal of the mist
that yet hangs darkly over the entrance to life's
closed and secret chambers. Man's dominion over
the earth will not be complete until he has fully discovered the secrects of its power and government.
The horse is his natural servant, ward, and companion, heading the list of the lower levels. The secret
of sexing once known, and the horse fills his place in
nature and becomes absolutely subordinate to the will
of his master. This little book will place him there,
not to make him physically more servile, but to make
his service the more valuable, because of his more
perfect subjection.

To these men, Messrs Barber and Slaughter, who
so unselfishly gave to me the entire managment of
this work, editorially and otherwise, I write most
cheerfully my grateful regards. And when I set them
forward to the world and associate with them Mr.
Coffman who will share in his place the honor of select
preference, I will be content to retire to my former ob-
scurity, and leave the trio to enjoy alone their well
merited glory. I promise however to follow this volume with another devoted entirely to the law of sex,
applied to the human family, and its power there.
This I mention in my introductory but is well in place
here. These two little volumes containing as they
will unmeasured worth to the world, I unreservedly
dedicate to the three names herein written, and hold
only the honor of subscribing, their editor and mana-
ger.   J. B. LAMKIN.
     Paris, Texas.

INTRODUCTORY.

For many long years there has existed a serious but very difficult question among the earnest seekers for scientific knowledge which has led them to ask: Is there a law governing the animal kingdom, or any part of it, by which the sexes are determined? And is this law known or to be known to man? Without question we admit that everything is produced and controlled by law, or by chance; and since such high order appears in all perfect physical motion, we are forced to decide against any "chance" theory, and proceed to answer the above questions with emphasis. There is a law by which sex is determined in the process of animal reproduction, and it can be known to man. Animal reproduction, or, "the bearing after its kind," is and ever has been of sufficient importance to hold the same in perfect continuance. It can never be considered irrational to hold that, it is radically wrong to hold a mere "theory," against known and stubborn facts. We know that like causes produce like effects. It is a fact that if we plant corn we will gather corn. It is a fact that corn will not produce potatoes. It is a fact that some law governs to prevent such occurrences. It is a fact that corn always produces corn. It is also a fact that there is a law by which this must be, and cannot be otherwise. It is a fact that each vegetable genus, is within itself, clothed with the power of continuance, when "surroundings" are favorable. It is also a fact that the "surroundings" are of law, as much as the power of racial propagation. Temperature must be at proper degree, treatment of proper order, and soil of proper nourishment, all of which is by fixed laws. It is a fact that species are derived from generic mixtures and law places to their extension a positive limit. This being true of the vegetable kingdom, can anything less be said of the animal? But in view of the fact that in the animal we find superior importance in some way, would it not of necessity occur that the law governing the latter kingdom exerts a correspondingly superior power? It is a fact that law cannot exist without order, nor can order be maintained without law. It is a fact that the male and the female of both the kingdoms named, must copulate at certain and fixed times and conditions to produce an offspring. It is a fact that in the offspring we have both the male and the female, and that, in exact accordance with the law as observed, or unobserved. It is a fact that the more perfect the law of reproduction is observed, the more perfect the offspring resulting. Coming now to the animal kingdom, it is a fact that from each genus we discover variations in symmetrical form, differences in weight, texture, color, mind, power, temperaments, motion, etc., in which is displayed the great law of universal diversity, which positively forbids any two objects, "though within the very closest generic embrace," from being an exact counterpart of each other. In this we see the supreme reign of a perfect law. Without attempting to follow this line of thought to the first and great cause of all law, it is sufficient for us, if by positive results we can reach the second or third or still lower causes, if, at the same time we can discover by actual experiment, that we have arrived at a safe phase, or character of the truth. That a continual and multiplied media of causation exists, and of necessity must be so, cannot be successfully denied. That the inclination, or position of certain planets or stars, relatively to each other exert a corresponding influence including the earth as is readily admitted, has given rise to all the astrological phenomena that has ever been offered to the world. That moons, or satellites, exert an influence upon the planet to which they belong, is not disputed in high scientific circles. That the earth's satellite or moon, positively produces great oceanic swell or tidal wave is true and the only known limit to this influence is the breaking of the wave on the eastern continental shores. Just what effect the moon's power after losing its grasp upon the great deep, has upon the land, has not as yet been accurately ascertained. But, that the moon influences both the animal and vegetable kingdoms on the earth's surface cannot be successfully denied. The "signs" of the Zodiac have long been recognized as in some way affecting the Mammal family and all such as have a determined, or defined nerve plexus. All this being true, and perfect order being preserved, positively forbids chaotic or chance events. In the entire classification of facts the one of sex certainly stands among the highest. Racial extension depends entirely upon it. This no one can deny. And if law governs perfectly the lower order of physical life, why should it be abandoned when it comes to that upon which all else depends? Such thoughts are absolutely absurd. The higher the object sought, the higher the law by which it is reached. If when Gallileo discovered the motion of the earth; Harvey, the circulation of the blood; Newton the force of gravitation; Morse the utility of the electric circuit; or Cooper the power of steam, if some scientist had discovered the secrect of sex, we would now be left to conjecture, as to which discovery would be entitled to the highest honors. But the secret has been discovered, not by an accomplished scientist. but by an earnest, industrious, investigating plebeian, who has given almost his entire life to experiments, and studious observations, to solve if possible, the sex problem. He now comes in this little volume to place his discovery before the world, but under such guards as are richly due such disclosure. The announcement of this discovery is not hastily or incautiously made. Feeling as he has for years, that the medical profession, together with the breeders of stock, and especially the breeders of fine, blooded, and imported stock, were all anxious to know the secret of sex breeding, or have a male or female offspring, just as the breeder des'red, would be gladly hailed, but with the severest test and criticism. Fearing lest his fortress might be stormed, the discoverer placed his secret in the hands of a well known and well indorsed breeder of imported and fine blooded horses and jacks of Texas, whose certificate and location will appear further on, together with a few of his staid patrons, who have been satisfied for years that some one had the secret of sex breeding, and who made many fruitless efforts to obtain it. The author of this article is well aware that this age of popular sentiment does, and of perfect right should demand facts before speculative theory, and especially will it be true in this matter of sex breeding. This volume will be devoted to stock breeding alone. And that part of sexual science relating to the human family, or breeding for sex there, will come forward in a separate volume; and the law governing the one, will there distinguish itself from the law governing the other. Hygenic rules with dietetics can be made to serve a high purpose in determining foetal health and character, but nothing whatever, with determining sex; which we trust we shall discover as we proceed to detail our sexual secret. To notice and attempt to answer the many theories advanced from time to time, by studious investigators, who have appeared upon the world's stage of science, and pay them the respect to which they are really entitled, would mean to prolong this introductory until it became of itself exhaustive and tedious, to be followed by a volume or volumes, unsuited to the restless, moving age in which we now live. We shall endeavor in this little work to be as brief as our subject will permit, and, as the public now demands, clothe our thoughts with as few words as possible, and thereby keep always directly to our subject. We shall bring forward some very important Bible evidence. Clearly showing that anciently the secret of breeding for sex was known and practiced in the family household as well as in the field, by which will be proven, that modern science, when it has unveiled this secret to the world, by its tedious, diligent, wonderful search and triumph, has only recovered a long lost art—that of applying a simple, natural law. If in this little book, or the secrets it contains, we can succeed in re-opening some long closed and obscure chamber in these temples of ours, and give back to the world that which is its own, we feel that we will have served a place and purpose worthy of much higher and grander beings than we are. We are well aware of the many theories appearing at different periods, and each receiving all, and many, much more credit than was due it, upon the great subject of breeding for sex. Some of the most popular I quote from a work entitled "Horse Breeding," by J. H. Sanders, page 64, under head of "Controlling the Sex." It has been said there is nothing new under the sun, and that each succeeding generation spends most of its time in shoveling over the same earth that has been examined in vain by its predecessors in search of hidden treasures. * * * That of controlling the sex of offspring has, ever since the days of Aristotle been one of the most fruitful topics of discussion, and the various theories that have been advanced, appear and reappear with perennial vigor. These theories may be summarized as follows:

1st. A strong mental impression on the part of the parents, but espicially of the mother, at the time of conception, will determine the offspring.

2nd. The concentration of the attention of the dam, on her peculiar qualities, at the time of sexual union, will secure female progeny.

3rd. If the amorous desires of the male are stronger than those of the female, the progeny will be a female, and, vice-versa.

4th. The development of the fœtus in the right side (horn) of the womb will secure a male and in the left side a female.

5th. The point of origin of the artery of the testicle from the main abdominal trunk (aorta) will determine the sex of the majority of the offspring, the male sex predominating in proportion as the origin is more anterior.

6th. The male germ is supplied by the right testicle or ovary, and the female by the left.

7th. The excitation of one side or the other of the system of the male at the time of coition, will determine the sex of the young.

8th. The persistent selection for breeding purposes of females which yield one sex mainly, and of males from females of the same kind will finally secure a race producing a great excess of the sex in question.

9th. In uniparous animals every successive ovum that reaches maturation is of the opposite sex from that which immediately preceded it. Hence by serving on the second occurrence of heat we may secure the same sex as in the last fœtus.

10th. The stage of development attained by the ovum at the period of impregnation, determines the sex of the product of fecundation, the less developed proving females, and the more mature, the males.

11th. The personal preponderance in strength and vigor of the one parent will determine an excess of its own sex in the progeny.

12th. The nature of the food of the parents and particularly of the mother before conception, will influence the production of the different sexes.

The theory that just now appears to be more generally believed in than any other is the 9th in the foregoing list. This based on the belief that, naturally, animals which usually bring forth but one at a birth will produce the sexes alternately, that, if the first ovum produces a male the next ovum if impregnated, will produce a female, consequently if a cow or mare after having produced a female is impregnated at the first period of heat thereafter, the product will be a male. If females alone are desired, one period of heat should elapse after the birth of a female before the dam is again served by the male. This is what has been known as the Stuyvesant theory, and many cattle breeders of my acquaintance, firmly believe that it can be relied upon in a majority of cases. Other theories have been advanced, but the foregoing includes the principal ones. It may be that several of these causes have some influence in determining the sex, but it is quite certain that some of them, notably, the 4th, 5th and 7th can have no influence whatever, and that none of them can be depended upon. * * * "

I introduce the foregoing theories and comments because of the careful thought Mr. Sanders has given to the subject of stock breeding generally, and giving the highest authority in bringing forward experiments in each particular phase of it. In view of the many very earnest inquiries into the mysteries of sexual science, and the successive failures of the investigators to answer correctly, the same author on page 66 of his work, exposes himself to a withering criti-

ticism by nature herself, by saying: "Nature has
wisely provided, in order to preserve an equilibrium
in the sexes, that their determination should be placed
beyond the control of any single cause." Despair of
ever knowing the law by which the sex was determined, or possibly to be controlled, may have prompted
Mr. Sanders to give expression to such thoughts.
Nothing less will apologize for the fallacy, since he
has not denied that all else as far as was then known
was governed by fixed and positive law. But appearing to recover from his disagreeable exposure, he says
on page 67, same work: "It may be that we shall ul-
timately discover the circumstances under which
these various causes operate upon each other, so that
we shall be able, in many cases, to produce a given
sex at will, but at present we know but little if any
more upon the subject than was known to our grand-
fathers. * * * " I bring these quotations forward in
my introduction because of the subject matter they
contain, bearing directly upon the law to be treated
of in the body of this little work, and to which I will
again refer. As a sequence to the tedious labor of the
scientest to penetrate the secret domain of the unknown, has the attention of the thinking world been
directed to the sublime intellectual altitudes, rather
than the sterner depths of pure plebeian thought, for
the unveiling of nature's deeper recesses. I grant the
logical righteousness of this, but at the same moment
protest, that, within this mundane sphere, we can
know anything more than nature as she reveals herself by fixed and immutable laws. With this view I
have no hesitancy in offering freely and fearlessly the
secret of breeding for "sex", as it comes from a crude
monument to nature's own genius. As the wonderful presence, pressure and power of gravitation became known by the falling of an apple, the utility,
power and motion of electricity by the subtile fluid

gliding down a kite string, the great strength of steam
by the lifting of the lid of a common tea-kittle, so has
come to light the wonderful secret of breeding for sex,
by the sight, and a desire to know the cause of an hermaphrodite. As in each case mentioned above, the
apparently limited suggestion, expanded with amaz-
ing power and speed, until now it is rapidly filling the
labratories of the world; we come now to offer another
and more astonishing suggestion by disclosing the
secret of breeding for sex, knowing as we do, how
long and diligently it has been sought. It cannot and
will not be denied, that under certain and peculiar
conditions and ifluences form, color and character are
affected and transmitted to progeny in both the animal and vegetable kingdoms, but just why and how
this is true cannot be known until some searcher has
disclosed the true nature of each individual's proto-
plastic elememt. That sight and sound does effect
the animal nerve, at any time, is an essential fact not
to be questioned. That the ovule, the spermatozoa,
the fætus, through gestation, and on to complete de-
livery and even later, is in continual contact with,
and becomes in a high sense the product of the material nerve, cannot be disputed. That a working hypothesis by which the relation between parent and
offspring may be clearly understood, has ever been,
and will perhaps remain, the closing act in the alche-
mists' dream, the very anguish of defeated speculative philosophy. We know that any substantial
progress in science is, and must remain impossible in
the absence of a working hypothesis, having a universal application to the phenomena pertaining to the
subject matter. And it can be truly said that until
such an hypothesis is discovered and formulated, no
subject of investigation can be said to be within the
range of the exact sciences. Kepler and Newton gave
the world an hypothesis from which has been formu-

lated a system, the exact working of which places astronomical measurements and calculations, together with the power and source of gravitation, within the domain of the accepted sciences. The Newtonian hypothesis did for astronemy just what the atomic theory did for chemistry. By the former the most intricate calculations are made, inspiring the scientist with perfect confidence, by the correctness of its results. The chemist knows that by combing oxygen, one part, and hydrogen two parts, that he has water. He also knows that to combine one atom, or part oxygen and one carbon, under heat, he has a deadly poison, carbonic oxide. But to add one atom, or part more oxygen, he has a harmless gas, carbonic anhydride, (dioxide) and so on throughout chemical combinations. The atomic theory can never be demonstrated by the geometric arrangement of the atoms themselves, and the chemist holds it as true only by results. Newton nor any of his disciples could demonstrate his hypothesis save by the correctness of calculations based upon it. Yet the scientific world is satisfied with both hypotheses and classifies them as exact science. In the great field of psychological investigation, a satisfactory working hypothesis has never yet been formulated. In a word, no theory has been advanced which embraces all psychological phenomena. Messrs. Bernheim, Braid, Sir William Hamilton, Dodd, Carpenter, Wigan, Dr. Brown Sequard, Proctor, Flint and many more learned and brilliant minds have invaded the domain of psychic phenomena, and in their struggle for a perfect, working hypothesis have given hypnotism to the world as a possible hypothesis leading through the field of psychic science. No working hypothesis has yet been formulated by which the physiologist can determine to a certitude the source, power, and life of atomic plasma; nor so long as it is absent can science claim to hold

the secret to the law of animal life.   Indeed if an hypothesis can be demonstrated, it is no longer a hypothesis, it is a fact.   If we knew the distance to the
sun or planets, or their exact dimension, any geometric theorem would pass into an actual fact.   And
the same can be said of any character of theorem.
A theorem may suggest a hypothesis, and vice-versa,
but no hypothesis or theorem are of any material force
when brought to face a demonstrated or actual fact.
In the treatment of a subject, however it may have
been presented, we can safely discard any theory
when the facts have been obtained.   The fate of an
hypothesis can always be said to depend upon the
character of its own logical deductions; in fact it must
live or die by them.   If the physiologist could formulate an hypothesis by which all the facts of sperm and
germ-cell life resulting from self or cross fertilization,
their perpetuity on the one hand, and their absolute
failure, or loss, on the other, could be fully explained,
or place us in full view of their genesis, then we
might well hope to obtain from such hypothesis the
perfect law of reproduction, which, as a logical sequence, would to a certitude determine the law of distinct sex, and by what exact process each are separate-
ly obtained.   But in the absence of such hypothesis
at present, the veterinarian and breeder will gladly
accept of a class of facts however small, and from
whatever source they may come if they will supply a
want, waiting so long for some philosophical development.   The fact of the many and conflicting theories
regarding the production of the two distinct sexes
from the same stock, is conclusive evidence, that thus
far, among the most careful and learned stock breeders, no working hypothesis has been formulated, by
which the sex of the offspring can be determined before the germ-cell has even been fertilized.   That the
germ and the sperm-cells must unite in order to pro-

duce an offspring, cannot be denied. But, that the
conditions of both or either of the cells, "per-se" determines their own character, and the character in
turn determines the sex, as is thought to be discovered in both plants and animals, is an uncertainty, upon which the most sanguine scientist may wreck his
fondest hopes. It would be useless to extend these
thoughts farther at present, but for the fact that theories have appeared proposing to solve the problem of
sex breeding based upon an hypothetical parity with
the astronomer, the chemist, and psychologist, when
neither nor all combined can become an hypothetical
parallel. Astronomical calculations are made minutely correct, without disclosing the deep secret of distance, power, and motion. The chemist obtains perfect results by an hypothesis based upon the unknown
power of atomic adhesion. The psychologist brings
forward astonishing results from the silent confines of
the "occult." But the physiologist finds his labratory filled with material organisms, bearing each material affinities, or material dissimilarities. The perfect
animal or plant, perfectly sexed, is of itself an absolute
theorem, the first and chief term in which proposition,
is a complete organized life. The second is like unto
it, produced by a perfect law—the first and the last
power in causation. The writer being absolutely ignorant of any case of self-fertilization of the germ-cell
by a sperm-cell of the same individual, he reasons
that unlike the process of flower fertilization, the
higher animal organisms become fertilized by specially fitted portions of each other. The hermaphrodite animal as contrasted with the uniparous or perfect unit, cannot be said to project itself so far into the
latter as to produce, contrary to nature's law, a sexual duality. Continued in and in breeding, so clearly
shown by Darwin, Huxley and Spencer, may without
exception among plants or animals, result finally in

the loss of sexual vitality, and yet never prove that
the sexual subsidance is due to anything but the violation of a fixed law.

From what has been said, and in view of the
high standard from which the subject of physical development and sex has been treated by the scientists
above named, we are the more inclined to think that
among the astrological phenomena to which at present so little attention is being paid, will come a sol-
vent for many of the problems appearing in popular
sexual science. I cheerfully endorse Mr. Darwin in
his own expression, as well as his acceptance of a
thought from Mr. Huxley, after duly considering the
crossing and re-crossing of flowers and the nature of
the hermaphrodite animal, that, intercourse with a
distinct animal is nature's legal necessity. It is well
known among bee-keepers that a queen once fertilized
by mating with a drone or male bee, is fertilized for
life, and the hundred-thousandth egg deposited by
that queen is as fertile as was the first one after mating. But no hypothesis has yet been formulated by
which this process, with many facts of fertilization in
plant and animal life can be fully explained. To say
that science will not finally unveil the deep secrets of
organic life, would provoke pity, rather than con-
tempt for its author. But that it has not yet done so,
cannot now be denied. Reviewing the last preceding
pages we see nothing forbidding the fact that the law
of time, being the only law that cannot be violated directly, has ever and must continue to govern the sex
in all organic life. And that the hermaphrodite oc-
curring in the higher animal life, is as legal as that
of a perfect sex. I cheerfully admit that the subject
of stock breeding in general, or by specific features
has been treated by far more profound and experienced minds than our own, yet from the unsatisfactory,
and undetermined effects of inbreeding, and the yet

undecided causes and true character of any or all
known injuries, I will ask, if continued inbreeding
depresses or dwarfs the progeny, where as has been
discovered uniformity of form or color has been obtained, why would or could not continued crossbreed-
ing be made to produce any desired size, weight, form
or color by giving especial attention to the qualities
of the animal or animals with which you cross, if
there was no positive legal limit to your operations?

By a close study of the law of psyshic phenomena, together with phrenology, after passing through
anatomy and physiology we come in close contact with
the horse and study him as we would study a man.
We soon discover that the horse has as well defind
temperaments as a man, and these operating by their
peculiar presence and combination, determine the
habits, character and strength of the animal. Mr.
Sanders in his book on stock breeding, under the
head of "General Principles of Stock Breeding," has
brought forward many very excellent thoughts, em-
bellishing his own with many splendid thoughts of
eminent authors, upon the same subject. The influence of Species, climate, changed conditions, habits
and treatment, he presents in a very interesting man-
ner, as each presents its peculiar effect upon the
horse, none of which we can afford to pass unnoticed.
Mr. Sanders leads us to understand that some one or
more of these influences are brought to bear in forming the general character of the horse; and also by
taking advantage of them, the breeder can and does
mould the character much to his own liking. These
thoughts suggests some facts, and some very interesting possibilities. If we could at any time obtain to a
certainty a pure speciman of pure breed in the horse
species, in the genus Equus, we could then begin to
study the real character of the horse. But subjected
as he has been to such a variety of climates, conditions

and treatments, that it is hard for us to know how
near we are to a pure, natural horse. But one thing is
very noticable throughout all these changes, improve-
ments and deteriorations, that the horse maintains an
equilibrium by some secret law, and he still remains
a horse. No one animal perhaps has been studied
and improved as has been the horse, which has been
due, no doubt, to the fact that a horse is a natural servant and companion of man. Strange however, the
horse having been so long a subject and ornament of
nature's labratory, that so little of his real makeup is
clearly known. Mr. Sanders cites many instances
and methods of breeding for some peculiar bloodstrain,
among which and perhaps the most important is that
of inbreeding as a means of obtaining and preserving
a desired quality. Now just a moment. The breeder for quality, selects such animals only as indicate it.
The animal must appear to be susceptible of receiving
the improvement desired. It must also indicate its
power to transmit to its progeny its own qualities.
Now what are those qualities, and how are they
formed? I have said that the horse had temperament
much the same as man, which are for our present purpose, the mental the vital, and the motive. In forming the character of the horse these temperaments take
on many modifications—viz: the billious, sanguine
and lymphatic, which take on a sub, or second modification, which is, the motive, mental, the billious;
motive mental, the lymphatic mental, the lymphatic
motive mental, the nervous mental, and the nervous
lymphatic mental. A third modification is only that
of the second. In this modification the mental pre-
dominates, and hence is said to be a modification of
the mental. The same is true of the vital and motive
these being the chief or grand temperaments of man
and the genus Equus. The function of these temperaments are, for the mental, intellect, mind, sensibility,

etc. The vital, vigor, motion, symmetery of body, clearness of mind and physical motion or activity. That of the motive, to give bone, its color, size, texture and character of muscle, blood, nerve and general physical strength. Combine these three in either man or horse and you have a perfect specimen. Their modifications always determine how far we are from our perfect specimen. The perfect draft horse take a modification making the motive chief. The Clydesdale, the English cart horse, and the Percheron, European importations, may furnish us as near a specimen of draft horses as at present is possible to obtain. The large strong bone, short heavy pastern, hard horny hoof in the pure bloods, coarse hairy cannons, coarse heavy mane and tail, the black, brown or bay color, are positive marks of the motive temperament. The slow or sluggish movement, the moderate ease of flesh, the weak or low swing of the upper eyelid, the small lungs, as compared with the weight of the animal, show the presence of a billious lymphatic modification, and the absence of the vital, a low mental, a sluggish and slow heart-beat, low excitability, are conditions suited only for draft purposes. If a draft horse is desired, the breeder will, in making his selections for breeding, attempt at least to combine as many known qualities necessary to his purpose as possible, and once united it becomes necessary to cautiously see that none are lost by crossing with inferior breeds. Temperaments determine the character of the individual, but not its species. Temperaments arise from the presence and combined powers of the vital organs, or forces of the body. Temperaments then become indices to the correspondence of the vital organs. In-breeding for a draft horse means to save a combination against loss by diverse breeds, i. e., against the vital motive first appearing to us in the pure Percheron, giving more speed. Reaching

the Cleveland Bay, a horse of rare value for all harness
purposes, we get a motive vital temperament with a
nervous flux in the vital, modified by the motive,
which gives the animal speed, power and endurance,
not to be wasted on adverse or lower breeds. Close
and careful, if not much, in-breeding is necessary to
preserve this combination, since it is true that by
what is known as heredities, effects a change in the
size, texture and power of the vital organs, and hence
a corresponding change in the temperaments. A
degenerated, or valueless, species means a degenerated process of breeding A perfect species, means
an unbroken or uninterrupted process of breeding
which fixes by hereditary molecular action in building
cellular tissue from which organic fixture arises, a
fixture in the temperaments, thereby giving a combination which of itself becomes organic and will remain
until interrupted by the infusion of a diverse combination from some segregated species. For a moment,
and for our purpose at this point, let us discard this
and form a new index. Could we closely examine
the physiology of the animal from which we now
desire a cross, we would glance at the blood, get its
color, the relative number of corpuscles, the red to the
white, its motion, volume and freedom from fetid
matter, which will lead us to the kidneys, liver,
heart, lungs and brain, the condition of all which we
will find as indicated by the blood. From the brain
we pass directly into the nerve plexus, following
along their walls, we visit every portion and organ of
the body, having gone through the genital machinery
and watched the blood as it yielded to the magnetic
touch of the two sexes, in nerve contact, rapidly
gathering plasmic life and forming a little, wriggling
spermal animal, and transmitting it to the opposite
electrode, a willing and ready receiver, an infinitesimal chamber with an open door into which our little

wriggler glides across the waves of a spermal sea, carrying with it and forming in its new home the temperaments as they are to appear in the life of the future animal. The strong and stylish cart horse, the nimble boulevard driver, the fleet trotting and race horse, each, if carefully bred, have a well defined nerve plexus, involving the vital organs in a process of manufacturing temperaments suited to their own peculiar use. When a desired breed is once obtained, its continuance depends upon how well it is guarded against adverse mixture and how long the one breed can be repeated until you reach perfect equilibrium. I mean equilibrium in the radial centres. If a temperamental quality is to be preserved—say a nervous, vital, mental—giving us the fleetest animal, and in-breeding is resorted to, to perpetuate it and father is bred to daughter, daughter to son, son to sister, sister to father, and so on, you will eventually reach an equilibrium which in some way becomes an absolute bar to further progress, and barrenness and sterility is the inevitable result. You will now ask what about this? The formation of the magnetic chrystal, or the positive and negative cones, are absolutely necessary to all life, both animal and vegetable. No plant or animal can live without these chrystals in some form or number. No chrystal can form where there is no magnetic or electric circuit. No circuit can be established where there is no attraction. There can be no attraction where the two poles are either positively or negatively electrified. In this case our poles are now repellants. This being true, the germ cell repels the sperm cell, and vice versa. It now occurs to us that there is no union of the two cells thus at magnetic equilibrium, and hence no offspring. Each of the cells thus repelled would become prolific when brought in contact with oppositely electrified cells. The earth gives the negative

chrystal, and its surroundings the positive. The
earth's satellite is a known magnetic excitant. The
inclination of the earth upon its orbit determining its
magnetic equator, and other planets in opposing
positions all operate as magnetic excitants—relative
positions, relative excitant—from which is obtained
magnetic motion. The moon, with its low temperature, becomes to the earth a high positive pole, and
being near it, eqerts a continued energy upon it, and
yielding, as it only can, a reflection of the sun's power
it must of necessity become the most potential agent
in forming the chrystal upon which all life depends.
From this view we discover why in-breeding, and in
fact out-breeding, where magnetic equilibrium is attained, as is proven by many striking instances,
results in apparent barrenness or sterility, as well as
to arise from some physical deformity. And possibly
many physical deformities for which no other satisfactory account can be given, may arise from either
physical or mental equilibrium. We will later on
learn how to breed for and preserve any quality desired and attained, when we have learned more of the
law that governs us. Another very interesting phenomenon is given by Mr. Sanders under the head of
" Influence of First Impregnation." The subject is
worthy of more than passing notice in view of the
many facts presented in an article by Prof. James
Law, of Cornell University, a very learned veterinarian. In this article Prof. Law presents the fact that
not only the " mare," but other domestic animals—
the cow, ewe, sow and bitch—are, quite a per cent. of
each species, contaminated by the character of the
" male " in first impregnation. The question, why
some young mares when impregnated first by a jack
then subsequently by a horse, will in the subsequent
foal exhibit some features of the jack? And so on
with the other animals. Prof. Law here quotes an

argument by McGillivray, who advances the theory
that some element or elements from the blood of the
fœtus by absorption contaminates the blood of the
mother who is never after of pure blood, and hence
incapable of producing a pure-bred offspring. Prof.
Law's criticism pronounces this theory the merest
assumption. He next quotes Mr. Darwin, who varies
slightly from McGillivray's theory and discovers the
blood filled with infinitesimal living, plastic or plasmic
germs to be gathered up and used when needed to
build up some character or condition in the animal
economy. These plasmic germs, Mr. Darwin argues,
pass through the membranes, the placenta and uteral
wall from the blood of the fœtus to the blood of the
mother, and circulate and multiply there by a rapid
process affecting at the same time the ovaries of the
female so that the ovules and offspring, when impregnated by other males and produced by her, are plainly
hybridized by the first male. Without offering to
illumine superior lights, I am inclined to favor Prof.
Law, and at the same time hold himself for the
absence of a single sunbeam touching the solution of
the problem. If Darwin's theory of absorption of
fœtal blood causing "sports" or variations in character of offspring should at any time obtain, it would
as quickly disappear under the fact of a transfusion of
blood from the veins of an animal into the veins of a
woman without in the least affecting her after progeny.
Why Prof. Darwin confines the function of the gemule
to the building of the fœtus, or embryo, or to hybri-
dize the ovule in process of development in the ovaries
and, against much logical argument to the contrary,
as is shown by Law and others, losing sight of a
more plausible theory, that of plasmic carriers, is a
little difficult to understand. If, by the walls of the
uterus, through the placenta, the fœtus receives its
nourishment from the mother, and that nourishment

is utilized in building a new animal, and the function,
or one function at least of the placenta, is both
stomach and lungs, and also that of all the vital
organs of the fœtus, and perhaps the lowest secretory,
the argument would be plausible that an exchange of
gasses, oxygen for carbon and vice versa, was contin-
ually going on between the mother and the fœtal
process, and this being true, it would be possible for
spermal gemule from the sire to be caught up in the
gaseous process and lodged permanently in the blood
of the mother, where with the native gemule it lives
and propagates and when called upon projects some
part of the parent imagery, and hence the " sport "
or variation following in the subsequent impregna-
tions.   If this admission of Prof. Law is correct, then
possibly, both Darwin and McGillivray are correct in
their absorption theory.   I will here ask Prof. Law.
Can there arise carbonic acid in the fœtus until some
tissue breaks down, or falls into disuse, or is rejected
in the building process ?   Is not the entire fœtal structure, from coition to parturition, a continual system
of joining molecules and not of tearing down and
carrying out ?   Is not this the " umbilical " function,
until the last wall is completed, or even the plexus is
tested for its magnetic polarity, or the mental helix of
the mother is placed in contact with that of the fœtus
or the nerve centre ?   And is this not the last work of
the mother, since nervovital fluid in complete circuit
must vitalize or stimulate to action the entire secretory system, necessitating oxygen by respiration,
which could take place only in open air, where, without injury to the mother, carbonic acid can be
exhaled, given off by the new machinery in its first
work ?   Is not meconium, or first effete matter, in the
embryotic intestine put there for the sole purpose of
establishing the digestive machinery in the mucous
membrane and prevent at the same time adhesion of

their walls until the cylindrical canal is complete?
Now, the mother being the sole builder, could not by
any hygienic process to either herself or young, afford
a redundance of material for the building, which
alone would necessitate the absorption process. From
this view appears some physical fallacy in the recipro-
cal theory, and still leave the mentioned effect of first
impregnation to be accounted for in some other way.
The writer is ignorant of any case of maternal
" marking " where the mother's objective senses had
not previously been affected. Leaving this thought
for a moment we listen to Prof. Law as he exposes the
Darwin theory of gemule transit from the embryo to
the mother's ovarium, there affecting all future ova,
and of necessity crossing all future progeny. But
Prof. Law, in attempting to shield his criticism, leaves
us in the fog by accepting the, to him, more plausible
theory of a mutual effect upon adjacent cells in the
womb and fœtal membranes and, confined there,
would not affect the blood of the dam, in future breeding. If the fœtal gemule is not securely lodged in
the uteral wall and there unchanged await subsequent
impregnation, nor passed into the circulation to await
there the next fœtal action, then it would occur that
the claimed effects are all false, or the effect is from
quite a different source. If in our search for the true
source of physical fœtal marks, we discover that they
originate either by heredity or maternal mental impression, the only question left for us is how to
account for and prevent the occurrence of so much at
least as is due to maternal mind. The case mentioned by Mr. Sanders of the black buck in his
father's flock of white sheep, is certainly a clear case
of impressed vision, which is but one instance of the
great number known to exist. The presence of the
black buck, so sudden and strange, produced mental
fright, with the white ewes possibly in various stages

of gestation, which fright so impressed their "senses"
as to convey color to the offspring. Now what
"sense" was thus affected? A brief notice and my
introductory will end. It has long been known that
many field and forest animals, and fowls as well, and
especially those well domesticated, are, in a very
high degree, subjective. This subjective sense resides within the motor nerve plexus. It receives
and retains impressions from the external or objective
sense. By stimulants, narcotics, fevers, frights and
passions, the motor cell is made to reproduce the
exact impression given through and by the objective
or external sense. These subjective projections mat-
erialize in exact accordance with the excitement under
which they appear. The strength or character of the
impressions is in exact accordance with the external
force that makes them. The sexual passion coming
from the motor nerve cantre returns with any impression it may have received from the objective or
external management. The sexual passion being a
determined excitant, and with the female seeking
and obtaining gratification in the male, if the male
have no peculiar mark in color or form by which
some special impression is made upon the now deeply
negative subjective female, the subjective cell now
closes with no other impression than the fact of the
sexual gratification, and hence the law of production,
acting without extraneous pressure, produces an offspring in regular order. But should the female
copulate with a male of peculiar form or color, and
this the first contact and hence first impression, hence
new nerve cell, she would in this case receive and
retain the deepest impression. Subsequent impreg-
nations are by reason of the same excited passion and
as a rational sequence, the second being to the female
a repetition or reproduction of the first, awakens the
first impression from its subjective slumber, with any

peculiar form or color, or even motion, of which it was composed. And the objective sense or mind being now perfectly passive in the female, her subjection now operates in full force and in the local centre at the moment of coition, now hybridizes the sperm cell, which in its hybridized condition determines the form, color, motion and mental character of the fœtus in exact proportion to the power of the subjective reproduction. I feel safe in saying that not a single instance of a "sport" or variation in the fœtus has ever occurred when, from whatever cause it may have arisen, with an objective female. I may be called upon to explain more in detail, which I perhaps will do in the work on sex breeding in the human species. But in more than a thousand cases in horses, cattle, sheep and swine, and among the various breeds, the writer has failed to observe a single clear case where a fœtal variation had occurred with a highly objectivized female. I have but briefly alluded to these questions of apparent abnormalities in order to produce a few parallels to the various theories of sex breeding, as they have appeared and reappeared from time to time and been exhaustively treated by profound scientists, without as yet approaching the real secret.

SECRET KEY TO STOCK BREEDING
FOR SEX.

We live in a day when the power of materializing facts is rapidly dispelling the vapors of speculative theory. Science and the Christian's Bible are locking hands to invade the mysterious domain of nature and nature's God. With this holy union, man will discover the splendor of his own being, and that of the power that produced him. It is said that knowledge is power. It can as truly be said that consciousness of power produces knowledge. Men disbelieve the Bible because of its claimed to be "formulæ" of the world's source and progress. To science, much Bible teaching has been and is yet but a complex hypothesis.

In this little volume we come to deal with some facts. Facts concerning the physical life of created beings. Our Bible teaches us that God said, in his genesis of creation; "Let there be light in the firmament of the heaven, to divide the day from the night; and let them be for signs and for seasons and for days and years."—Gen. 1-14.

"And God said let the earth bring forth the living creature after his kind, cattle and creeping things and beasts of the earth after his kind, and it was so."—Gen. 1-24.

"And God blessed them and God said unto them be fruitful and multiply and replenish the earth, and subdue it, and have dominion over the fish of the sea, and over the fowl of the air, and over every living thing that moveth upon the earth."—Gen. 1-28.

It could be well said that when Moses wrote these scriptures he lived in a day and with a people who knew that the sun and moon in some way determined and controlled the day and night, and also the stars, for they were lights in the so named firmament. As to who and how the knowledge, that the lights determined the seasons as well as the day and night, appeared, may not be clear to us, and just what Moses meant when he said so, may not be fully known until we have learned all the secrets of animal life. Whatever else Moses knew of astronomy more than the length of the day and night, and moon's phases by observation, he, without doubt knew something of the astrological secrets as practiced by the Egyptian astrologer and magician. Moses understood well the meaning of God's command when he said replenish and subdue the earth. We can hardly see how man could place the earth under his control until he had well studied the means for doing so. And especially would it be difficult until he had learned the secret law of his own life, by which alone could he subdue himself to himself. And until this was done, not only with himself as a part of the earth, but with the next higher order of animals, which were to serve him for a higher purpose, could he be absolute monarch. We admit the correctness of the scripture statement of God's injunction to all living to bring forth after its kind, which if left undisturbed it would continue to do without man's legal assistance, while then as now, the passions governed. But the higher injunction to man to subdue all the earth would evidently mean that the work would not be accomplished until man so controlled animal nature that he could make it bring forth to his own suiting.

Science at the instance of its diligent and competent disciples, is apparently approaching the secret of hybridizing with both plant and animal, and will

no doubt discover the law of blending there as is now
so clearly shown with the mineral kingdom, in the
laboratories of the chemist. We do not claim that
the Bible affords a special formula to us by which we
can at a glance obtain the secret of breeding for sex,
but that we can gather some clear inference, that sex
breeding was understood and practiced by the an-
cients, we think will clearly appear. Astronomy of
the nineteenth century was not the astronomy of four,
five or six thousand years ago. The "science" of to-
day is the fruit of a system of fine arts in the "long
ago." Whatever of the artistic was then practiced,
and has since been confirmed by scientific analysis,
can now be said to have been empirical. But as must
be conceded by the most devoted disciple of modern
science, empiricism has often paved the way, or maintained in its crude practice, some very high status of
scientific development. Without following this
thought further at present, I will resume my approach
to the real purpose of my work. By reference to
Ecclesiastes 3:1 we get an expression ascribed to Solomon; "To everything there is a season; and a time
to every purpose." Eccl. 3:2; "A time to be born,
and a time to die." 8:6 he says: "Because to every
purpose there is a time." From the scriptures I have
quoted, Mr. Slaughter inferred very naturally, that,
coming as they did from the wisest of men they could
not be made to speak their full meaning, and not
comprehend a full knowledge of the "time" to bring
forth a male or female offspring. The fact that old
scripture genelogies teach us that from the beginning
of the age of man, the first born of every family, and
in almost every instance two, three or four, at least,
of the subsequent births were male children, forces
us to acknowledge that these old families were favored
through successive generations with a very singular
class of accidents, or they knew of a time that sexual

intercourse would produce the sex desired. When we discover from the long used form of national government, being the lineal or family form, the head of the family, the father, ruling, and this the only form, and upon the man so much depended, we are inclined to the belief that even in that remote age the law governing sex was well understood. And in addition to this, when we are forced to admit, that in all nature, there is not a known physical production or motion resulting from mere chance, or just a happen so, but on the contrary, we see everywhere a reign of law, we are still the more inclined to this belief. And can we not very safely say, that when Solomon said there was a time to be born, he meant he knew there was a time, when a male or female could be produced according to the wish or purpose of the producer? And can we not insist, that he knew full well the time to copulate, since by Israel's genealogical tables, and his own knowledge of man's superior worth, and the importance of Israel especially, keeping his genealogy pure, that he not only knew of a time, a proper time to copulate for sex, but by what unerring influence the sun, moon and stars exerted over man and animals? And we are led still further in the belief that Solomon not only knew the law governing sex in the human family but also among the beasts of the field when he speaks with so much emphasis as touching the termination of organic life indicated in Eccl. 3:18-19-20-21. * * * " And that they might see that they themselves are beasts. For that which befalleth the sons of men befalleth beasts, even one thing befalleth them: As one dieth; so dieth the other; yea, they have all one breath; so that a man hath no pre-eminence above a beast for all is vanity. All go to one place, all are of the dust, and all turn to dust again. Who knoweth the spirit of man that (it) goeth upward, and the spirit of the beast that (it) goeth downward to the earth. "Solomon knew full well that the organic properties of physical man and physical beasts were quite similar in their nature and combination, and the simple fact of form, and intellect, gave to the one no advantage over the other. If we now begin where Solomon dismisses his vexed and dual simile, and pass back, which we can well do, and say with him that all are alike in death, all are alike in life, all are alike in organic elements; hence all must be alike in their birth, in the primary planting for a birth, all alike in the time to plant, similar in the passion that prompts the planting, and all in some way alike in diversifying sex and of necessity there is a law by which all the physical properties of this dual simile are held in place, power and motion. In extending our thought until it embraces more fully Solomon's meaning when he teaches us that he knew there was a time to all things and the same supreme rule applied to the vegetable kingdom that so perfectly governed the animal. We hear him in Eccl. 1-2: "A time to plant and a time to pluck up that which is planted." Anticipating some one's answer, that Solomon only meant that which any sane person will concede, that, with the animal, birth and death could not take place at one and the same time, joy and sorrow, pain and pleasure, grief and happiness, anger and docility, hatred and love, were incompatible powers and influences. And to the vegetable, the season, springtime, time to plant, summer to grow, and autumn to gather, or as the latitude would indicate, so act, was all he meant. Can we at all acknowledge the superior wisdom of Solomon and at the same moment make him squander it in such pure plebian expressions? Wisdom may utter her voice in simplicity, but her every effort is to place the pupil upon a higher plane. But wisdom defeated, musingly utters her own lamentation by the power of

KEY TO BREEDING FOR SEX.

so great a contrast, as to her alone can appear, and in such words: "As it happeneth to a fool, so it happeneth even to me, and why was I then more wise? Then I said in my heart that this also is vanity."–Eccl. 1-15. Viewed from a certain plane Solomon in common with any philosopher, decided it was foolish to be wise, but neither can or could at any time say it was wise to be foolish. So we must conclude that the time to plant seed in the earth to which Solomon refers, was to the future plant, as the time to copulate was to the future animal. Resting our thoughts at this point for the present let us introduce the "moon," the earth's satellite. As will appear in our proofs, the lunar month is divided exactly into two equal parts, commonly known as light and dark or new and full moon. Counting the exact length of a solar year we have 365d, 5h, 48m, 48s. If in perihellion and perigee the earth's and moon's inclinations were exactly the same to the plane of their orbits, giving an exact day length through the complete orbitular circuit, and the moon's path had no orbitular variation, the exact length of a lunar month would be 28d, 2h, 17m, 36s, and the solar month 30d, 10h 15m, 32s. One half the lunar month so counted would be exactly 14d, 1h, 8m, 48s, which would be the time given each to the old and new moon, or in rural lore, the dark and light moon. Let us at this point say with assured candor, which will appear in our proofs, that to the full moon belongs the male, and to the new, the female sex. The so-called waxing of the moon is from new to old, and the waning, from old to new. The decreasing, or waning moon, fitly represents the male. The vigorous power and greatness of the man, while in the full strength of his masculine glory, is but the monumental splendor of a fixed and unalterable waning, so strikingly displayed to us in the full moon, whose silver face neither sparkling nor brilliant, shows no life nor light that is not borrowed. And while in the zenith of his glory he looks with soft and charming gaze upon his enchanted, admiring minions, he silently waves them his sad adieu, and slowly turning his jeweled face, his steady waning so surely passes him out of sight. The increasing or waxing moon just as fitly represents the female. Coming as she did, and yet does, from the unconscious slumbering of man's wasting fullness, she appears the decorated delicacy of a superior and splendid ruin.

Her beauty now increasing,
Her attraction now unceasing;
All nature bows and yields to her embrace,
Held within the enchanting power of her face.

With the facts that will herein appear we can very safely say to science; no longer scout the rustic claim, that the "moon" really has to do with both the animal and vegetable kingdom, and that its influence there is in some way an all important factor. A question might here be asked, why has the moon a path around the earth? Why do we have light and dark moon? What is meant in God's decree that the lesser light should rule the night, and that the stars also should take part in the great influential relation? It will be clearly seen that this very mention indicates that there are relative solar forces existing that no member of our planetary system could afford to loose. And that there was some kind of planetary alliance, appears evident, from the ebbing and flowing of the tide. With these and kindred thoughts and interrogatories Mr. Slaughter began with these few dim lights before him, to explore the regions of the unknown, a search for the secret of sex. The fact that the sexes were about equally divided, and that perfect sexing was the rule, suggested to him that there was a law somewhere governing this grand equation.

Laboring under many disadvantages Mr. Slaughter began a close system of observations among the farm stock. Noting the date of the foal of the mare, he observed that the first heat after foaling expired on the twelfth day. Counting back nine days would bring on the first period of heat on the third day after foaling. This, where the mare was healthy and did well in foaling. When the mare was not bred in first heat, as a rule she would be in heat after the twenty-first day after foaling. This heat would last from seven to nine days, and go out about the twenty-eighth day after foaling. But if bred in either heat, he observed the time the heat expired in which impregnation took place, whether in the new or old moon. Following this to foaling, he began to discover that if the mare was bred in the old moon, or that the heat expired in the old moon, the foal would be a male. On the other hand, if the impregnation heat expired in the new moon the foal would be a female. Here another question arose, which was all important. How many days belonged to each moon? And did they follow or precede the moon? To determine this, his observations had, necessarily, to be very close. He here observed that if a mare was bred the three last days next preceeding the full moon, and the impregnating heat ran six days into and including the day the moon fulled, the offspring would be a male. Also if the impregnating period terminated any day after the third day, after full moon, and one day before the change or new moon, the offspring would be a male. Mr. Slaughter further observed, that it would be safe to breed as far as the fifth day after the full moon, supposing this to be the first day of the heat, for it would then terminate one day before the new moon having had then, nine days to run. Observing and applying this rule the result was invariably a male offspring. He then applied the same rule, and closely observed the result, to the new

moon, and in every case the offspring was a female.
These closely made observations settled in his mind
that the full moon controlled the next succeeding
fourteen days including the day of fulling, and terminating one day preceeding the day of change, or
new moon. He also observed the same, *i e*, that the
new moon governed the next succeeding fourteen
days after and including the new moon. Mr. Slaughter's attention was called, early in this sex-breeding
search, to the question of barrenness in the female and
sterility in the male, deformed wombs and the hermaphrodite. He knew all these questions had been
quietly resting with physicians and horseologists, under the almost unanimous decision that they were
only freaks of nature. This did not satisfy him, and
he asked himself, what is a freak of nature and why
do they appear, and in so many ways? And could
we not know if the freak was the merest chance, or
the violation or distortion of some fixed law? Mr.
Slaughter was keeping, and kept, his search pro-
foundly secret for more than twenty years, choosing
to make a slow progress, if progress he could make at
all, rather than risk evoking criticism and ridicule, in
case his search was fruitless, or have but a small share
of the glory in case he succeeded. And being a man
of retiring, plebian habits, this course to him was not
difficult to pursue. But the questions above enumer-
ated still remained to him vexed and difficult, and the
more so, when in a casual way he would put them to
some skilled physician or veterinarian, and be
answered, only a freak of nature. And to the question of sex, it was just a kind of happen-so. With all
these evasive and unsatisfactory answers from grad-
uates in anatomy and physiology, Mr. Slaughter was
not dismayed. The conviction that surely there was
some key to the mystery held a persistent influence
over his mind. The hermaphrodite among the do-

mestic animals was really the first cause of his search
for the solution of the great sex problem. At the age
of fifteen years Mr. Slaughter for the first time saw a
hermaphrodite. It was of the human family and
quite young enough that the circumstances of its birth
were sufficiently vivid to furnish Mr. Slaughter,
though but a boy, a basis from which to begin to
reason. His first question, why this double sexed or
non-sexed being? Why did its nature permit this?
Was it law, or no law? Why were there not more of
them, or none at all? And were they in any other
physical way affected? Was the only visible deformity
in the procreative organs? If so, why so? It had a
strong sexual passion and no possible way to gratify
it. If this was a mere freak of nature, was not nature
in this inexcusably cruel? Were the parents in any
way responsible? Delicate as were his questions, Mr.
Slaughter learned that both were properly sexed and
at time of copulation were not in any perceivable way
unduly influenced. Mr. Slaughter, young as he was,
was so impressed with this "freak" that he determined to know the true cause, if it was possible to
obtain it. He was then living with his parents in
Giles Co., Tenn., and he applied to the most skilled
physicians of his county to explain; but to to his surprise they said in answer to his questions, they did
not know, it was a freak of nature. But did these
physicians know all that could be known of this peculiar freak? The boy said, there is a correct answer
and I will get it. He applied to other physicians and
learned men, but as often received the same unsatisfactory answer. He used the little advantage he had
with books, but to no success. Gathering up the old
legendary practice of planting certain crops "in the
moon," and seeing, as he thought, some decided effect, he reasoned that if the moon had this influence
upon the vegetable kingdom, why did it not in some
way affect the animal? And if so, would not or could

not, the question of sex be known, and settle his hermaphrodite problem? Two other hermaphrodites came under his notice, one in the horse, and one in the swine. By close inquiry he learned that the breeding of the mare that foaled the hermaphrodite colt was done right on or very near the dividing line between the two moons. But did this decide anything; if so, what was it? Hermaphrodites were too infrequent to furnish him the sole material for his study. Now if he could decide the question as to whether the moon in any way controlled the sex, from this hypothesis, he could determine the appearance of the hermaphrodite. And might it not also prove that the direction in which the scientific world had been looking for an understanding of this phenomenon, was not the right one? Firmly beleiving he was in the right path, Mr. Slaughter continued taking notes during the breeding season, noting the day the foal was dropped and counting as a rule the twelfth day after foaling as the end of the first heat. Should a mare be bred in this heat, and prove to be in foal, in which moon did the heat terminate? In these cases, and there were enough of them, where the mare was bred and impregnated in the first heat, to get satis-factory data, that the first heat terminating in either new or old moon, did without failure determine the sex. To repeat here what I have already shown, and which appears in our diagram, that in the cases just named, where the twelfth day of first, and impregnat-ing heat ended after full and before the new moon, the foal was a male, but, if terminating after the new and before the full moon, the foal would be a female. Following with these observations into second, third or more heats, in every case where the impregnating heat terminated in either moon as above stated, the result was the same. Feeling sure that he had thus empirically discovered the secret of breeding for sex,

Mr. Slaughter turned his attention to the hermaphrodite with some assurance that he could learn something definite of its nature and cause. Reasoning from
the facts appearing in his hypothesis, if the full moon
conception determines the male, and the new moon
the female, was there not a point somewhere between
the old and new, or new and old, where there would
be no sex, or be both? This seemed to him so plausible that with renewed anxiety he sought more and
additional data from which he could obtain some reliable proof. Mr. Slaughter had, by close study and
observation, learned enough of the hermaphrodite
index, as written in the face and body motion by
which he could determine who was a hermaphrodite,
whether in male or female attire. While a young
man he chanced to form an acquaintance with one in
female attire, and taking its place as one of a circle of
fashionable young ladies. He courted an intimate
acquaintance with this "young lady" for the purpose,
if possible, of making or having made a close exami-
nation of her, or its person, that he might learn as
nearly as possible the exact nature of the deformity.
Learning as he did for sure that she, it, was a hermaphrodite, he pursued his purpose until by mutual
consent, he had permission to make a thorough ex-
amination. In this case a small vaginal cavity was
found in or near the proper place for a female, and
terminating abruptly at or near where the "neck" of
the womb should be in a well sexed female. What
was above this closure to represent the uterus, or the
ovarium he did not minutely determine. But the fact
that no menses appeared and no symptom of retention
was perceptible, he inferred that the ovarium was as
incomplete as the uteral cavity; which would argue
that there were no defined ovaries, no fallopian tubes,
no uterus, *i. e.*, nothing defined, and hence no female
sex. Searching for the male procreative duad, he

found no testicles, no penis other than a small protuberance, apparently nothing more than a protruding clitoris, which was of no perceptible use as the urine was voided by the vaginal cavity. Mr. Slaughter further learned that the sexual passion was very strong, almost incontrolable, and quite continuous, and no visible means of gratification. At this point quite an important feature became very noticable. The face had no well defined masculine marks to a casual observer, and especially when treated to a cosmetic coating. The absence of the male procreative organs, the choice of female attire, and preference of young men for social companions, convinced Mr. Slaughter that this was a case where ovum maturation occurred· with the mother exactly on the new moon, having descended from the ovarium in the old moon, which act will be taken up later on. At this time Mr. Slaughter was closely following his hypothesis, and of necessity was forced to rely, as will be clearly seen, upon the strength of a logical theory, which to him must stand until disproved by facts to the contrary. Before proceeding further we will try to exhibit by suitable plate or diagram, a lunar month showing the old and new moon with the days belonging to each. and the exact point at which conception takes place, to give a perfect male and a perfect female, a slightly deformed womb causing barrenness, and a dormant genatile organism causing sterility.

In following Mr. Slaughter's hypothesis through this plate or diagram, I would not for a moment attempt to lead an intelligent public to believe that he could, or would attempt to account for all procreative abnormalities by this hypothesis, knowing as he does that there are many malignant impediments to breeding, arising from diseases of the procreative organisms, among which I will name: Overfeeding either mare or stallion; fatty degeneration of the ovaries;

DIAGRAM.

	FULL MOON.	NEW MOON.	FULL MOON.	NEW MOON.

SEC. 1.

1 ooooooooooooooo
2 ooooooooooooooo o
3 ooooooooooooo o
4 ooooooooooo o   o
5 ooooooooooo   o
6 ooooooooooo oo

1—Barren female.
2—Female hermaphrodite.
3—Hermaphrodite.
4—Male hermaphrodite.
5—Sterile male.
6—Complete male.

Half lunar month, 14d, 1h, 8m, 48s.

SEC. 2.

†
1 ooooooooooooooo o
2 ooooooooooooooo o
3 ooooooooooooooo o
4 ooooooooooooo o o
5 ooooooooooo   o o oo

†—Sterile male.
1—Deformed male organ.
2—Hermaphrodite.
3—Hermaphrodite female.
4—Barren female.
5—Complete female.

Half lunar month, 14d, 1h, 8m, 48s.

SEC. 3.

1 ooooooooooo
2 ooooooooooo o
3 ooooooooooo
4 ooooooooo
5 ooooooooo

1—Female.
2—Hermaphrodite.
3, 4, 5—Female.

Half lunar month, 14d, 1h, 8m, 48s.

SEC. 4.

1 ooooooooo
2 ooooooooo
3 ooooooooo
4 ooo
5 ooooo

ooooooo
oooo

1, 2, 3—Male.
4, 5—Female.

Half lunar month, 14d, 1h, 8m, 48s.

stricture, or muscular closing the neck of the womb; deferred breeding long after maturity of the mare; expulsion of the semen from the womb by spasmodic contraction at the moment of coition by undue or over œstrum, or heat; fatty degeneration or blocking of the fallopian tubes, preventing the descent of the ovum for impregnation; over-work, or over-strain with either mare or stallion, an undue exudation of mucous from the uteral wall, induced by protracted obesity, or too rich food, etc. But that a class of non-productions and deformities of the procreative processes do arise from our hypothetical exhibit, will be stoutly maintained while facts continue to appear.

The dots in our plate represent days. The dotted line at Fig. 1, Sec. 1 gives the entire fourteen days belonging to the new moon, but terminating at the outer disc of the full moon where the change is taking place and is too far complete to accommodate a union, in fact cannot retract. The sperm cell, impregnating by its union this non-sexed germ, or partially changed germ cell, produces from this ovule a barren female.

Fig. 2, Sec 1 makes the fourteen days terminate within the disc of the full moon, the change being still more complete produces at this point an hermaphroditic female. I mean as much the more a female than a male as the ovum lacks of reaching this lunar meridian at the exact time of maturity.

Fig. 3, Sec. 1 passes the dots or days to terminate directly on this lunar meridian, where the subsidance of the female is complete in the equilibrium here produced by the first, or incipient male influence, and the closing or maturing ovum receiving the sperm cell and is impregnated, produces a dual sex condition, which can now produce only an hermaphrodite, or a unit of two non-sexed duads.

Fig. 5, Sec. 1 begins the fourteen days one day after new moon, and terminates one day after the old, crossing the disc, and giving one day on the outer rim at a point too near the meridian to have a complete male ovum, which if impregnated in this condition the product will be a sterile male.

Fig. 6, Sec. 1. This terminal point is now two days across the moon's disc, and should a mare be bred this second day, and that the last day of her œstrum, or heat, the sperm cell of the male is now in contact with a mature ovum, and if impregnated, the offspring will be, all else being equal, a well sexed male.

Sec. 2 is a full moon period, a period for maturing male ovules. The † shows us the near approach to the new moon meridian of the fourteen days allotted to the full moon, and terminating near enough to this lunar meridian to unsex the ovule then maturing, having descended nine days before, and which if impregnated, will produce a sterile male. But if it should not come in contact with a sperm cell it would pass out and be lost.

Fig. 1, Sec. 2 terminates at a point sufficiently within the influence of the new meridian, or tristing point, to affect the sex of the ovum, now maturing to the close, but still approaching nearer the determined sex line to affect the genitile organism and produce a sexually deformed male.

Fig. 2, Sec. 2 terminates exactly on the new meridian, at which point a change from the male to the female influence affects the descended and mature ovum, as in the case at full moon meridian, but from male to female, and if the now non-sexed or double sexed ovum should be impregnated the product would of necessity be a hermaphrodite.

Fig. 3, Sec. 2 passes across the moon's disc and places us within the moon's shadow, and at a point where the ovum will mature more to the female, having now entered the gate to her enclosure, than to the male, and should this ovule be now impregnated, as is shown in Sec. 1, Fig. 2, the product would be a female hermaphrodite. From this it will now be seen that the male and female hermaphrodite can both be produced on the same moon and within a few hours of each other, by one maturing on one side of the lunar meridian and one on the other. We have now shown three distinct points on the moon where rests the possibility of producing a hermaphrodite. But we may here be met by some one with the question; will the number of hermaphrodites bear to the total number of births, the same ratio that the time as shown in the diagram for making the change on the moon's disc, bears to the entire time elapsing between the two lunar meridians? I can at present only answer that, to formulate an hypothesis by which we can, or could minutely and accurately account for the entire class of maternal sexual deformities, i. e., those present at birth of the young animal, would be to claim a perfection in our formulæ not expected to develop from one so young as ours. But so long as our reasoning maintains a logical parity, and is supported by existing facts, there is no opposing hypothesis, less supported, to which we would willingly yield. In the absense of a correct concensus of the hermaphrodite and hermaphrodite animals, we will assume, having no reliable data at hand, that the ratios when accurately obtained, would demand no better explanation than can be found in our diagram. In the absense of any positive information regarding the maturity of the ovum, whether, as a fixed rule, it takes place in the ovarium proper, in the ovaduct, or in the uterus, we can very safely make this statement; that owing to the many known obstructions to ova descent, that a mature egg may be found in either locality named.

Fig's 1 and 2, Sec. 3 is explained in figures 1 and 3 in Sec. 1.

Fig's. 3, 4 and 5, Sec. 3 are the nine œstrum, or heat days of the mare, which are embraced within the days of the new moon, and conception taking place on any of these days will insure a female offspring. If a foal is dropped one day before new moon, as a general rule, the mare having twelve days in which to have her first heat, she can be bred on the seventh or ninth days, provided she is impregnated, and insure a female offspring.

Fig's. 1, 2 and 3, Sec. 4, are all within the days of the full moon; and within one, two and three days respectively of the close on the coming new. But a foal dropped twelve days preceding either close, will insure for the mare a male for the next foal, if she is bred and impregnated on either of these days, and it will be, all else being equal, well sexed.

Fig's. 4 and 5, Sec. 4 show the crossing from one moon to another of the days of heat, arising three, four or five days preceding, in this case, the new moon, which if on any of these days the animal is bred and impregnated the offspring will be a female, and all else being equal, will be well sexed and prolific. I feel sure in closing this explanation of the diagram, that the breeder will now make no mistake in his work, and if he follows the instructions closely he can have a male or female just as he may desire. In passing on across our field of search and discovery we will frequently refer to our diagram and will endeavor each time to give the breeder something of value to his business.

RESUME OF OVUM MATURITY.

Let us assume that the ovum is not projected from the ovary until mature, and at the moment of maturity is detached or expelled from the oval chamber, and begins its descent through the ovaduct to, and down the fallopian tube, stopping at the uteral wall to await further orders. Here let us ask; did the expulsion or detachment of the mature ovum bring on œstrum or heat? If so, why as a rule does it come at regular periods? Can food, condition, habit or care produce such regular order, since in neither do we find a system so complete as is here suggested. Or does the beginning of the heat determine the expulsion of the ovium, and its descent acting in conjunction with the progress of the heat, it slowly but grandly glides along its bridal avenue, arranging its toilet, decorated by the "new" to become the bride, or jeweled by the old moon to become a bridegroom? If the maturity of the ovum determines the heat, and it descends for the sole purpose of propagating its race, and impregnation should on any account be delayed, then we argue that the defeated egg must return to its former state or continue the heat indefinitely. It now very clearly appears that the œstrum, periodical as it is, is determined by an influence not residing within the capricious elements of the immature egg. And further, if the egg is mature at time of expulsion, and its voyage is for the sole purpose of impregnation, and the heat is for the sole purpose of inclining the animal to the service of the egg, should impregnation take place the first day of œstrum, the now fertilized egg would take its place in the fallopian tube or return to its uteral chamber, and the heat then and there terminate. But this process is not so conducted. By every indication perceivable the whole procreative process, both work and machinery, are governed by time in a system of signals, which if not obstructed, proceeds in perfect keeping with the importance of its work, and divides and subdivides its time so that each generative maneuvre, in continuous and quick succession, gemules laden with protoplasmic atoms build tissue and cell, and at a moments warning signal their completion. At this point let me ask, where does conception take place, and at what time? Properly the place is in the fallopian process, but may vary by muscular pressure or nerve condition, serving to prematurely open or spasmodically close its fecundation cavity. It is contended by many veterinarians that conception, or the complete union of the sperm and germ cell, takes place at the moment of coition, and the uniparous ovum, admitting one only, spermatozoon, closes its door, and at once begins its uteral attachment, and by muscular action the womb proceeds to expel the seminal surplus, when the work of fecundation is completed. Others, that meeting as they do in the upper uteral chamber, the spermatazoa falls within the oval embrace and is retained there until the ova has made itself ready for the cellular union, which when done closes instantaneously. By the terms of our hypothesis, conception cannot take place until there is mature ovum, and notwithstanding copulation may take place at any time after œstrum begins, conception will be deferred until the ovule, as in the case of plant life, is mature. We hold with the facts obtained that as a legal act the ovule descends or is projected from the ovary, nine days prior to maturity. The projection depends upon the œstrum. The œstrum depends upon the moon. Two heats and one rest period or one heat and two rest periods to one lunar month. The detached ovule is furnished with nine days rations from the ovaries. This wandering ovule must capture a spermal prize or starve after the end of the nine days. The ovule is not mature when expelled. It is expelled for the purpose of maturing. When once mature its sex is determined, not by any intrinsic element or power, but by the law of time that matures it. Nor is it sexed by the sperm cell from the male, for it has no power over it save that of fertile life. As we have shown a high and inexorable law governs, the law of time. The spermatozoa, in the semen of the male at copulation carries sufficient spermal plasma to feed

the impregnated ova which is done at the exact time
of maturity, until it is attached to the uteral wall, its
embryotic home. From our lunar meridian we will
now begin our minute division of time, and see if we
can find support to our hermaphrodite exhibit. By
the U. S. census of 1890 it will be safe to say that we
have one hermaphrodite to each 100,000 horses and
mules, which estimate is too low unless we confine
our count to that class of hermaphrodites that have
an equal development of both sexes, or having two
positive sexual duads. But coming as we must from
this exact sex meridian, through the modifications,
embracing both barren or sterile animals, arising
purely from this lunar cause, and we can raise our
estimate until we would find one in 1000. This being
in any sense true, we can at once see that we are
given sufficient time to cross the moon's disc, and al-
low every ovule maturing there to be so affected.
Our astronomers calculate the time of full and change
up to the minute. Their reason for doing this arises
from the fact of there being an exact point at which
the moon's position to the earth and the earth's inclination to the sun are each changed in degree, and
the moon being so near the earth that the effect of the
change of degree, minute and second, being known
in count of time, would argue that it would also be
felt magnetically. I feel that the thoughts here
brought forward are sufficient to place the subject of
the hermaphrodite among domestic animals sufficiently clear before the reader. In our recapitulation
at the close of this volume we will try to rearrange all
these lights. But remember, to our credit, we regard
ourselves only pioneer in a very wonderful work
awaiting the profundity of the coming scientist. We
are now to give some observations upon some other
effects of the law of sex. The question is often asked,
why among uniparous animals do we have twins,

triplets, etc.? This question would seem at once to come well within the fixed terms of our hypothesis. Whatever speculation may be indulged, we have some facts from which to predicate our deductions. If, as we have seen there can be no impregnation without mature ovum, a projection from the ovary, and descent to the fallopian duct. This being true, it is also true that a fallopian condition as already mentioned may obstruct the passage of a mature ova until it is overtaken by an immature one, and the two or more as the case may be, will descend together at the moment of coition, which in the case of a voluptuous prolific female, is accomplished by relaxation of the nerves and muscles by the heated pleasure of sexual contact. Spermatazoa and spermal fluid now sufficient, impregnates the mature ova, and the immature ovum, embracing as is its function, spermatazoon and spermal food holds it until it is mature, at which time without segmentation, they begin and complete their voyage to their uteral home where they are nourished and perfected by the same placental process. But will our hypothesis give us the reason why one is a male and the other is a female, as in the case of twins? Easy enough. The first ovule that matured, did so, if the male, in the old moon and near the change. The second, descending later, matured in the new and hence a female. But you will answer is it not true that many pairs of twins, and occasionally triplets, are all of one sex? Yes this is true, but being true, does it argue that it just happened to be so, or an undefined freak of nature? As we are at a loss to find a "single" happen-so birth, the same would also be true in the plural. Without entering into the plasmic production of the ovule, or the exact function of the ovary, by any known theory, we are safe in saying at least, that two or more ovules may be projected or thrown into the

ovaduct at the time, and together with their separate
cells, descend for impregnation, which by time of maturing and conception, in either old or new moon,
both be either male or female as per diagram. I will
say at this point, there being no logical argument to
the contrary, that our hypothesis is well supported by
facts, and what would be true in a single birth would
be equally true in plural birth as to the law of determining sex. In the majority of plural births one or
the other is barren or sterile. Some one might attempt to answer this by spermatozoidal exhaustion.
We are not prepared yet to receive this, for we cannot
appreciate just how the male could project a prolific
and healthy sperm cell, and well sex one germ cell,
and fail to effect another, at the same time, knowing
that impregnation is determined by spermatozoa from
the semen, in which they are found in sufficient numbers to impregnate more than one with a fertile organism, a sexed condition, if sex depended upon the
action of the ovarium, or the seminal ejection. Our
hypothesis determines the sexing of the pluro-birth,
as well as the sterility or barreness of either.

We may just here indulge a theory of oval con-
version, and not in any respect wound or weaken our
hypothesis. Should it prove true that the ovaries, in
their spontaneous production of ova, in and of themselves produce or manufacture gemules from some
gaseous material element, and of the gemules thus organized and vitalized, produce ovules and each ovule
modeled after the manufacturer would primarily have
the female form, and escaping from a ruptured ovisac,
now become subject to some influence, which of
necessity resides without the maternal organism, if
that influeace, power or fixed law should, of the same
identical ovum change completely its sex once or
twice in each month, transforming the female organism with its corresponding members, to that of the

male, and vice-versa, and not of necessity destroy the
ovum in the process nor even permit it to become detached until it had undergone repeated changes, in
fact, continued subject to such changes while it remained within the ovarium, what valid objection
could be urged against it? What if it should be discovered that prior to maturity the ovule is absolutely
non-sexed, and presents to the eye of the examiner a
material susceptibility only to a regular sexing process by which the susceptible parts are, by our hypothesis, converted by our determined lunar law, into
whatever sex produced by our lunar periods, what
objection could be urged against that? This may, to
the casual observer appear the merest speculation,
and yet eventuate within the range of some term of
our hypothesis. Whatever digression we may seem
to make from our diagram or exhibit, we will not,
cannot destroy, or even weaken the facts as already
shown by it. In dismissing these speculative thoughts
we come to examine another important feature in our
work. It is known to any observing stock-breeder,
that during the breeding life of a mare, there are some
periods of heat more fervent than other periods, without any perceptible change in flesh, habits or other
surroundings, and for which he has not been able to
account. By close observation Mr. Slaughter discovered the fact that, all those periods of high heat in
mares, jennets and cows occurred on the full moon,
and also the lower or more moderate heats came on
the new moon. He also discovered that a mare bred
in high heat and impregnated and foaled a male offspring, seemed much more docile, less irritable, and
more agreeable among other animals, and easier every
way to manage. These facts of high heat on full
moon, a male offspring, docility of the mare in after
life, led Mr. Slanghter to examine more closely old
scripture genealogy. I should perhaps have made

necessary exceptions to Mr. Slaughter's hypothetical ruling in the above citations, but I have made them all through this work, and I trust the rational reader will observe them here.

The fact that there is not a genealogical household mentioned in old scripture that had not a male child for its first-born, from Adam to the birth of Christ, and even much later, with the fact of the large majority of births among cattle, sheep and goats along the sacrificial ages, became of much interest to Mr. Slaughter, the close study and watching of which confirmed Mr. Slaughter in his new discovery and satisfied him that the secret of sex-breeding was a practical art and was well known to the "ancient of days." Mr. Slaughter's attention was, in addition to the scriptures already mentioned, called to the inauguration of the sacrificial service in the Levitical priesthood. Beginning with the first chapter of the book of Leviticus we discover that God is very specific in describing the character of the sacrifice, its relation to the magnitude of the offense or purpose for which it is made. It is clearly seen in this chapter of Leviticus, the third chapter and forty-first verse of the Book of Numbers, with the thirteenth chapter and twelfth verse of Exodus, that of cattle, sheep and goats, where the sacrifice was for any congregational purpose, God required it to be a firstling, a male, and without blemish. Nor anywhere throughout the law, or any allusion to it by any prophet, Christ or his apostles, is it intimated that the sacrifice could be otherwise and be acceptable to God. To Mr. Slaughter these sacrificial qualifications, added to the fact of a male child being the first-born of every family, argued by their very nature that the art of sex-breeding was known and practiced by those old time families. And not only did they of those ancient days understand when to breed for sex, but how that this first-born male should be without blemish which meant to them as also it means to us, a perfect birth. No one who will closely read these scriptures can for a moment deny that in some way a very superior art or custom governed both farm and household in their practice of reproduction. If but occasionally in house or field the first-born was a male, the fact of this might offer a very plausible apology for the joy and celebration of the event, when their ritualism depended so much upon it. But this was not true. As we have shown by scripture reference that a male first-born was expected as confidently as was the birth, and their joy and celebration of the event continuing with these genealogical triumphs, and their repeated allusion to the Lord, in these victories, as being in some way the author of their continued precision, leads us more to think those people were not only familiar with the law of sex-breeding but their knowledge of it came to them in the same way in which they had obtained the entire law. Our attention is here directed to the case of Elisha and the Shumanite; 2nd Kings 4:15-16. The prophet here clearly expresses a knowledge, which in no way was connected with his calling as a holy seer. But as he felt a duty toward the wife for her care for him, and willing to perform it toward her, he ordered her into his presence and plainly questioned her as to what she would have him do for her. The servant of the prophet gave him her wish and words as she had delivered them, which added to the prophet's knowledge of sex and what influenced it most. In this case, as we have given in general indications of sex control, the prophet knowing the woman was childless, and that a barren womb was no credit to any one and also that the time to conceive a male child was the time when the sexual passion was the highest, and her confidence in the man of God, acting as an inspiration, prompted her to say

she was childless; and her apparent doubt of the
prophet's sincerity was but the expression of an anxious hope. When Elisha said; about this season, according to the time of life, thou shalt embrace a son,
and no expression of surprise or wonder at the prophet's knowledge coming from neither the servant nor
the woman is but positive proof that all of them knew
that it would be as the prophet had said, and not be
out of the way of a known ruling law. We get some
further thought on this same subject from the expression of the husband of this woman as found in the
23v of this same chapter: "Wherefore wilt thou go to
him to-day, it is neither new moon nor Sabbath.".
Now why did he say this? He knew not of the death
of the son, and he, the son, being large enough to go
to his father in the field, and to talk plain, we would
infer that the husband supposed his wife desired an
interview with the prophet regarding another child.
We further infer that as the first-born was a male,
that it would be no breach of family custom for the
next child to be a female, and as it was by the inspiring presence of the prophet that the first conception took place, that it was as a sequence of the first,
necessary for the wife and prophet to be in each
other's presence for subsequent conceptions. We further infer that the husband and wife had mutually
agreed that the second birth should be a girl, that
they might have one of each sex, and the more since
we clearly see that chances were all against them for
a family of children, she, the wife, very late to bear
at all and the husband growing old, is to us convinc-
ing that they wanted a girl next. Now we hear him
express surprise at his wife going on that business as
it was neither new moon nor Sabbath. Some additional thought arises from the Book of Numbers, 3c,
50-54v. "And the Lord said unto Moses; 'number
all the first-born of the males of the children of Israel.'

And thou shalt take the Levites for me instead of all the first-born among the children of Israel; and the cattle of the Levites instead of all the firstlings among the cattle of the children of Israel." While as we have said, there is no scripture clearly defining the law governing sex-breeding as we have in this work delineated, we claim the benefit of an inference as clearly drawn as many other accepted scripture doctrines and "facts." We now feel safe in saying that with more than a hundred scriptures in both the old and new testament to clearly favor us, nothing appearing yet in philosophic reasoning nor any scientific analysis to the contrary, together with these more than thirty years practical experiment and observation, our hypothesis will stand an impregnable fortress against sceptical criticism of the coming ages. It has not been our fear that this little work would be a failure in any of its essential features, or that it would falter when subjected to a crucial test for any number of years that caused us to offer it the support of these scriptures or any attempted logical or scientific argument. But believing that this singular production would be read by a large number of our best thinking people, we have been induced to offer some thought leading us back through the Bible to discover one of its most splendid customs, arts or laws, which has not come to us by either history or tradition. As will be seen before closing this little volume, we are not dependent upon any theory of science, formulated or accepted philosophy, scripture nor anything written or taught or even known prior to the experimental life of Mr. Slaughter for the stubborn facts as they appear recorded upon these pages. And while without hesitancy we can safely declare all this to be true, we are not so selfish even of the very high honor of making one of the world's grandest discoveries as to attempt to rob another age and another people of equal if not

superior honors.   Nor do we believe as Mr.   Sanders
suggests in his work, to which frequent reference is
made in our introductory, that nature has and is purposely concealing the law by which sex is determined
to prevent intrusions upon her prerogatives, and the
destruction of sexual science itself, but to the contrary we believe and earnestly maintain that so great
a trust as the great Creator reposed in the power, life
and wisdom of men, as the subjugation and managment of all the earth's productions would or could be
done only by committing to him the right to know
and apply the law by which he could govern it.   Nor
can any one justly charge us with a rude invasion of
forbidden ground nor of unlocking or attempting to
force an entrance to any secret chamber purposely
closed against us by the great Creator.   We well
know that quite a per cent. even of the reading public seem to think, and speak with some assurance,
that God never intended for us to pass beyond some
imaginary limit, to know only as it is written by some
predecessor, in fact they place an embargo virtually
upon the laws of their own life, by which they an-
nounce unconsciously more the depths of a profound
ignorance than the free and prudent altitudes of intellectual motion.   I have alluded to Exodus 13:12-15
as in some way offering strong support to our hypothesis.   And this scripture so admirably does so,
and comes so clearly within the range of preceding
thoughts that it will be well in place to quote ver-
batim: "That thou shalt set apart unto the Lord all
that openeth the matrix, and every firstling that com-
eth of a beast which thou hast, the males shall be the
Lord's * *   therefore I sacrifice to the Lord all that
openeth the matrix being males, but all the first-born
of my children I redeem "   We have alluded to
scriptures only relating to male firstlings of the flock,
and now in further defense of our hypothesis we offer

some scripture relating to the female offering. The reader will here remember I have said that in all sacrifices with blood-letting, the important or weighty ones were always made with a male, young, and without blemish. It will clearly appear from the reading of Exodus 4: 28 that minor offenses are expiated by blood, but the blood of a pure female is sufficient. In the Book of Numbers 19c and beginning with the 2v we have a very important statute established by the burning of a heifer, the ashes of which are kept for a special memorial to the end of the law. But it will be seen that this heifer must be without spot or blemish nor having been yoked. Now let us present a brief summary and examine it by our hypothesis. In all the scriptures to which I have alluded the sacrifice, whether of cattle, sheep or goats, were to be young or of the first year and without blemish. Mal. 1:14 tells us that God will not be deceived in an offering, it must be without blemish or his curse will be upon him that offers. In Matthew 19:12 the Savior teaches us a lesson we cannot afford to loose, while it comes so clearly within the range of our hypothesis. This scripture reads: "For there are some eunuchs which were so born from their mother's womb and there are some eunuchs which were made eunuchs of men." We understand the eunuch to be a male without testicles, and so born as it often occurs, in a horse, we call him a riglaud, or having testicles he is sterile or a male hermaphrodite. Born without the testicles showing it was in some way put upon an equality with castration. Castration then was a blemish classed with sterility. Barrenness was a blemish classed as a shame, cursed was the man with his seed in his belly. No man could approach the altar with broken stones. Lev. 21:20. Nor have any part in the congregation of Israel. Deut. 21:1. Now you may ask, what will you do with your little

summary? Our hypothesis brings this thought vividly
before us. If the blemishes here named disqualified
the animal for sacrifice, and the sacrifice had to be
made, and made of the firstling of the flock, and in
each case of a pure sacrifice it was to be of the first
year, we see at once it was a moral impossibility for
them to ascertain correctly at that age their proceative
purity unless they knew the law and the time conception took place that the first-born might be pure,
and the necessity is the more apparent for them to
know the exact time for an imperfect male or female,
since the divine pronunciamento was against any im-
perfection. Some one may say the male genital organism would exhibit the sex, condition very young,
so the priest would take no risk in making an imperfect offering. Admitting this to be true, we are met
by an imperative law that all that openeth the matrix,
meaning evidently the first fruit of the womb, and
this of every beast they had and this should without
variation or mistake be given to God, and a male and
pure, stands of itself a strong argument that they of
divinely made necessity well understood the sexing
process.

Mal. 1:14 adds a valuable thought along this line
and bears directly upon our subject of sacrifice and
teaches us that sure sexing was held as a dying tradition, and yet he reminds Israel that God would
curse a deceiver at the sacrificial alter, in his attempt
to offer a corrupt thing. I would not risk repeating
Malachi's warning to Israel were it not so far down
the ages through which, by the dim signals we have
cited, had been kept and practiced one of the world's
finest arts. Another reason for repeating this reference arises from the superstitious expression of a class
already mentioned, who regard any pioneer thought
as an invasion of God's private dominion. To that
class these scriptures present the fact that not only

did God not forbid or in any way obstruct a clear knowledge of sex-breeding, but severe penalties are pronounced against them when atttempting to make their sacrifices without it. It is now very plain to us by our perfectly harmonious hypothetical formula that we have before us a resurrection which will in no wise antagonize any expressed will of the Creator or force back upon the world an unused, unwelcome, or dangerous practice. Without dwelling longer at this point than to get a fair understanding of our subject as viewed from the sacrificial altar I will present Jacob among the field animals of his father-in-law, and see him as he applies a "knowledge" which he appropriates to his personal, pecuniary or commercial advantage. The casual observer of this little financial scheme of Jacob is liable to lose sight of the cunning precision with which he performed it. Jacob well knew by the established custom of his people, and the near relation of Laban to his family that he would have in every way a very decided advantage of his uncle when he had fully made known to him the object of his visit. Nor can we put any financial scheming beyond him when we so plainly see how he took advantage of his old and blind father and of his own brother when he so adroitly stole his brother's blessing. From a close reading of the little scriptures given us we infer that Jacob left his father's house with nothing more than was necessary for his journey and visit to his uncle. In a word he was a poor young man and his uncle had what we would now call a fair stock rancho. Rachal, Laban's daughter, was the only promised compensation to Jacob for his next seven years' work, at the end of which time he would have the girl and seven years' experience with his now father-in-law's flock. At his option he could then take his wife back to his own family or remain a hireling with Laban. We here discover Laban in a

little scheme ending in the sale of both his daughters
which at this time appeared to be the sole reward for
the diligent and prosperous work of Jacob on the
farm. Rachal was the debt Laban owed to Jacob but
deceivingly paid it with Leah. Jacob murmured but
was soon reconciled in the promise of Rachal at the
end of Leah's week and seven years more work on the
ranch. This proposition Jacob willingly accepted.
But why did he so willingly do so? Let me ask, as
appears in the sequel, had not Laban's flocks and
herds increased from the beginning under Jacob's
care? Did not Jacob know just why so many colors
had appeared among them and justw hat had produced
them. Does not the cunning of the man, beginning
with Esau and his pottage, tell us that he would not
with two wifes on his hands, his poverty, and the
promise of God to make of him a great nation, and
possibly begin it with these two women, have so
frankly told Laban what his wages should be and how
determined, without knowing to a certainty just how
to conduct the propagation, and how to speck, streak
and ring them up that he would get all the best of his
father-in-law's flocks? In other words how he could
rob him and do it in a business-like way, which is to
this day a well known commercial characteristic of
his descendants, and not know the exact methods and
law by which the marks were produced. It was evident from the very nature of his proposition that he
was not just at that time beginning a series of experiments not knowing whether they would terminate in
success or failure. But to the contrary we are the
more confirmed in onr belief of Jacob's "sexual"
knowledge of field life when we see him of his own
will divide Laban's flock, the varigated from the solid
colors and taking none of either as his beginning, but
only the chance of producing for himself in the future
his part, from the effect of his secret methods upon

that part of Laban's flocks that was free from rings, streaks or spots. We are further assured that Jacob knew well the secret power of his methods when he mixed and crossed his rods in the water troughs. We know as a common experiment that a little agitation of the surface of clear water so breaks the refraction of light that a straight rod under the surface of the water can be made to take on the form of spots, curves, steaks and rings, and at the same time appear to be moving in the water, which produces an effect upon the female when drinking at certain periods. This Jacob knew and knew just when that period was. He knew so well his work that he produced his desired effect upon the best of the herd nor could he afford to miss a single chance as there was just one time for him to put in sure work and that was in conception. This scripture presents us with a thought that may embody a very important fact. A question remains yet unanswered among the most learned veterinarians as to the exact time conception takes place, whether at the moment of coition, the end of the heat or at the maturity of the ovum. We feel sure Jacob knew just when his water vision would have the greatest effect and he evidently presented it at the right time. Judging from our experience with the custom of farm stock, copulation does not take place, except in very rare instances, at feed or watering time. Jacob could not afford to trust to a caprice of chance when the entire execution of his design depended upon his water trough scheme. As an historic fact this scheme of Jacob with Laban's flocks and herds, their increase coming exactly to his suiting, rapidly and surely absorbing all the good, his rapid increase in wealth as an undisputed sequence, stands up to-day without a parallel. Reference is often made to this scripture event as a pretty nice little game for a young Israelite, without realizing in the least its source, magnitude and importance. Not in the history of our race, except in the life and person of Jesus Christ, do we find such knowledge of the laws governing animal reproduction. If there be any truth in this account at all, and we are not prepared to dispute it at this time, we have the fact that Jacob's birth and life was far out of the ordinary. Rebecka, his mother, was barren. Isaac, his father, knew of her barrenness and that it was of a subtle nature. He appealed to the Lord for the healing of his wife. Her first conception was twins. One had the skin of a beast, but the brain of a man of clear intellect. The other, Jacob, indicated his cunning from his mother's womb. Esau came first from the womb, which by custom gave him a birthright, which meant a prior right to paternal favors and blessings, the right of the first born. Jacob embraced an opportune moment to purchase his brother's birthright, which he did, and by a little cunning conspiracy aided by his mother, executed the liberties of his birthright purchase in the little kid skin and venison game, by which was inaugurated the most remarkable system of national ethics the world has ever known. Whatever casuistry would appear, of which might be predicated Jacob's harmonious relation to his God, we just as certainly entangle both Jacob and his God in a very cunning deception, when Jacob was approached by the murmur of Laban's sons, or he overheard them complaining that Jacob hath taken away all that their father had and from it had gathered all his glory. Some perplexing thought is suggested to us in the reading of this 31st chapter of Gen., after reading the last twelve verses of the 30th, or preceding chapter. These Syrians, Laban and his sons, seemed not to understand Jacob's unparalleled success, and yet, as clearly appears in their willingness to covenant with Jacob when they had overtaken him as he was so stealthily leaving them, that his success during his six years' service for himself was no ordinary streak of luck, and Jacob knew they were now completely bewildered as he related to them how God protected him against their deceptions and change of wages, which meant that Laban thought to cut off Jacob's chances by saying just the spotted should be Jacob's, and when this was true then all the good ones were spotted, and God made it so specially to protect Jacob and this was true of all the marks. Now why did Jacob persuade these Syrians that God was maneuvering this phenomenal success and that an angel told him in a dream that the sires of the flocks and herds, as shown him in copulation, were ringstreaked, speckled and grizzled and that he could not change the run that everything had as it all went his way? Why did Jacob gather up his all and so secretly move out, contrary to the custom of family partings? And why much else just along here, all of which is so contrary to what appears, while he is fixing and carrying out the terms of his service contract? And why did he conceal and never mention or intimate his watertrough scheme? Let us take a glance at the situation and see if we can discover anything in favor of our hypothesis. We will assume that Jacob knew the secret of proper breeding for sex. By this assumption he secretly practiced, with other successful coadjutants, this law or method while caring for Laban's stock during his fourteen years' service for him. That he did not in any way disclose his secret nor any part of it to any one during these long years. That his purpose as shown in all his false ascriptions to God and his angel was to conceal from these Syrians a system, the secret of proper breeding for sex, which belonged to a lineage of which he, Jacob, was a divinely favored member. Saying nothing of Jacob's sincerity, that this account does not say, we are left

to face the plain fact that Jacob clothes his Labanic
debut in a sublime deception having no equal; and
no apology save in commercial Israel. If Jacob was
not a most consummate scoundrel, he was certainly
true to his secret, himself and his people. As already
indicated our inference is clear that Jacob knew just
when conception took place. Recurring upon this
thought, it was not necessary for Jacob to know the
anatomy of the procreative organs, their cell life, em-
briotic and fœtal life and development, in order to
know just how to obtain any desired effect. But that
he apppears to settle the question that conception does
not nececsarily take place at the moment of coition,
but as appears couched in our hypothesis the maturity
of the ovum determines conception, and not the heat
pleasure or contact in copulation, is evident from his
confinement of his materials to one place, and that
where copulations were quite infrequent. If it was
true that conception determined the time to place a
mark upon the fœtus or embryo, and it was at the
moment of copulation, then Jacob would as surely
have put his rods and poles at the breeding places and
not confined them to the watering troughs. So were
the thoughts of Mr. Slaughter, while he so studiously
conducted his observations and experiments, the facts
of which we now have notwithstanding many so-called
scientific assertions to the contrary. For the present
we will pass from these scripture references back to
the sphere of our hypothesis. A question of much
interest to all stock breeders, the keeper of the stallion
as well as the owner of the mare, presented itself to Mr.
Slaughter in repeated failures to impregnate, where
there was no real cause apparently for such failure.
Mr. Slaughter discovered that in the great majority of
such cases the heat period ran its full nine days. If
the mare was bred at the beginning of œstrum, or
heat, and the period lasted its full time, it was possi-

ble for the animal to be impregnated by first service
and returning to the horse the seventh or ninth day,
still being in heat, is served again to be followed by
another service on the next seventh or ninth day.
Was it not possible that something wrong could be
done by too frequent service or by serving the second
time in the same heat. Mr. Slaughter reasoned that
if conception took place at the maturity of the ovum,
and the ovum matured as the heat subsided, it would
of necessity occur that the second service coming in
in the same heat, came just at the time of uteral attachment, and the second service served only to destroy the then possibly well defined embryo, leaving
the mare unimpregnated and perhaps so to run
through the season. In this way Mr. Slaughter determined that many failures, so thought, occurred and
with experienced stock-breeders. His next question
was, how could this be obviated and not loose too
much time in the breeding season. He reasoned that
if each œstrum or heat matured an egg, and the periods were as a general thing but nine days apart, if
the breeder would, after the first service, wait eighteen
days before teasing again, his mare would, if impregnated at first service, go entirely out of heat, and not,
all else favorable, be in heat again through the season. If to the contrary the mare should fail to be impregnated at first service, by the eighteenth day you
can be sure, except in cases where regular monthly
heats run to foaling, that the mare is not impregnated.
If the mare should be in heat on the eighteenth day
and the horse serve her, then wait eighteen days
again before teasing. But if the mare refuse on the
eighteenth day, wait ten days before teasing again.
Should the mare be in heat on the twenty-eighth day
and the horse serve her, wait again eighteen days,
and so on through the season. The result of these
observations was to Mr. Slaughter and all others who

followed his instructions, very satisfactory. I know several good stock-breeders who follow this method with all their patrons, and will breed no other way, claiming their horses and jacks get more mares in foal, *i. e.*, their books show a higher per cent. of mares served to be in foal than under the old system, which is by far the most satisfactory to both parties. I have already treated of barrenness in the female and sterility in the male, arising from their various causes sufficiently, not to appear in this place. I make this last mention from the fact that some mares not really barren are uncertain breeders, which uncertainty may in the main be due to the custom of breeding every seventh or ninth day, or twice in the same heat. There is another very common obstruction to impregnation, and which when discovered is in most cases easily overcome. I speak of the contraction or spasmodic stricture of the neck of the womb, fatty blockading of the ovaduct, etc., which is all described and treated by veterinarians generally, but would be entirely out of place in this little work. I gave notice that some strong certificates would appear in the proper place in this volume, from men who had thoroughly tested Mr. Slaughter's method of stock-breeding, or proper breeding for sex, and perhaps it is proper to introduce them here. The first is from Mr. George Coffman, Anna, Collin County, Texas, who has for many years been known as a breeder of fine blooded and imported stock, and who would not permit his name to apeear in this work as an indorser were the facts not as are here given. This certificate was given to the editor of this work by Mr. Coffman at his home on the 24th day of May, 1898, and reads:

I hereby certify that I am at present a breeder of fine blooded horses and jacks and have been for many years, handling imported stock, and have used the

Slaughter method of breeding for sex, on my farm
and given its benefit to a large number of my stock
patrons, a few names of whom I give below. I have
used this method continuously for the last twelve
years, and in not a single instance where my instructions have been followed has it failed.

GEO. COFFMAN, Anna, Texas.
HAMP RATTEN, MELISSA, Texas.
NED MULLIGAN,   "   "
I. N. STEVENS,   "   "
R. POWELL, McKinney, Texas

We next give a sworn statement of Mr. G. W.
Evans, Emmett, Chickasaw Nation, bearing notaries
seal under date of June 18, 1898, and it reads:

To WHOM IT MAY CONCERN:—This is to certify
that I have followed the instructions given me by Mr.
R. M. Slaughter in his secret of proper time and
methods of breeding stock and in every case the result has been in perfect accordance with his instructions.   [Signed] G. W. EVANS.
Sworn to before J. T. Gardner, notary public, same
date.

Another satisfactory test by D. W. Norman,
Troup, Texas, which we give below:

TROUP, TEXAS, June 30. '98.

To WHOM IT MAY CONCERN:—This is to certify
that I have followed the instructions given me by Mr.
R. M. Slaughter in his secret method of stock-breeding for sex, and in every case the result has been in
perfect accordance therewith.

[Signed] D. W. NORMAN.
Sworn to and subscribed before me at Troup, Texas,
this 30th day of June, 1898.
[Signed] T. B. COLLIER,
In and for Smith County, Texas.

Below is Mr. Slaughter's own affidavit, and reads:
Be it known that I, R. M. Slaughter,. have for
the last thirty-eight years, been experimenting and in
every possible way, testing my method of breeding
for sex, or how to obtain a male or female offspring
as we may desire. I am now in full possession of the
method by which this can be done with perfect success, a true description of which is fully set forth in a
litle work entitled "Key to Secret of Breeding for
Sex," written by J. B. Lamkin, which work has been
under my supervision from beginning to end, and the
statements therein relating to time and method of
breeding are true and correct.

[Signed] R. M. SLAUGHTER.
Subscribed and sworn to before me this 6th day of
July, 1898.

[Signed] R. F. FRENCH,
Notary Public of Nida, I. T.

We could with some trouble and a little delay in
our work, add more names to our list of indorsers, but
while each certificate or statement would of itself be a
strength to our work, they would be but a repetition
of what we have given, and I am sure that by the
known integrity of the men whose names appear
herein, this volume will go to the stock-breeding
world as a production and a guide without a parallel
or rival in any age, or among any people save with
that of empirical antiquity. We have presented no
claim of science, as in any way as yet entitled to the
honors couched within the iron grasp of known and
proven facts. These we offer with all the stubborn-
ness and independence of their peculiar nature. I
have said that of all I have offered as theory, speculation or argument, something of which will remain
perhaps after the hardest strokes have been made to
crush it, there is nothing there upon which I would

depend for support in presenting to the scientific
world a work like this. If these theories had been
my dependence for proof, however well my hypothesis
might have been formulated, I could not have lifted
my hand and bid defiance to the scientific world, but,
with that assurance belonging only to the peculiar
nature of stubborn facts, I can say with becoming
modesty that we have nothing to fear from any source
while our structure stands on a granite base. To
briefly recapitulate will be to close this little volume.
As a universal law time determines and controls all
physical organization and life. There is a time to all
things. The earth, moon and sun give us time. The
sun, moon and stars constitute the power that forms
and governs sex. From one day after full moon to
one day before the new, determines the male sex.
From one day after the new and to within one day of
the full moon, determines the female sex. The
moon's meridian, either new or old, or the exact time
of change, determines the complete hermaphrodite.
The last waxing minutes of the new give the female
hermaphrodite, and the first waning minutes give us
the male hermaphrodite. Within a lunar month is
embraced the law that gives the breeder the perfect
male or well sexed male, the imperfect or sterile male,
the perfect or well sexed female, the imperfect or
barren female, the male, female and complete hermaphrodite. With this brief review of our diagram
we deliver to the breeder the only sure method of
breeding for sex the world has ever known. We can
with frankness and candor say if he will follow the
instruction here given, he has within his grasp the
power to have his barnyard stocked with either male
or female just as he may desire. As to the value
this little work will prove to be to the stock-breeding
world it would be impossible to estimate. The breeding of cattle as well as horses is embraced within our

diagram, but requires closer watching as the heat ebbs and flows more rapidly. We will say this, however: If a bull calf is desired breed your cow on or after full moon and as quick as you discover your cow is in heat. If a heifer calf, then breed on new moon as per diagram, and lose no time as it is known the cow goes out of heat when she lies down and chews her cud. We have now completed this litlle volume. In delivering it to the breeding public, we do so with a conscience void of offense, feeling that whatever the price paid for it may be, its value cannot be estimated by it, nor is there a page between its lids that does not in some way teach us of the majestic grandeur of our God, and the splendid dignity of creation, and that of our own being.

THE END.

www.ingramcontent.com/pod-product-compliance
Lightning Source LLC
Chambersburg PA
CBHW021528270326
41930CB00008B/1138